Queens of France

by Thornton Wilder

A Samuel French Acting Edition

SAMUELFRENCH.COM

Copyright © 1931 The Wilder Family LLC. All Rights Reserved.
Cover Design by Gene Sweeney.

QUEENS OF FRANCE is fully protected under the copyright laws of the United States of America, the British Commonwealth, including Canada, and all other countries of the Copyright Union. All rights, including professional, amateur, motion picture, recitation, lecturing, public reading, radio broadcasting, television and the rights of translation into foreign languages are strictly reserved.

ISBN 978-0-573-62432-2

Samuel French, Inc.
45 West 25th Street
New York, NY 10010

www.SamuelFrench.com

> For Production Inquiries
> Info@SamuelFrench.com
> 1-866-598-8449

No one shall make any changes in this play(s) for the purpose of production. No part of this book may be reproduced, stored in a retrieval system, or transmitted in any form, by any means, now known or yet to be invented, including mechanical, electronic, photocopying, recording, videotaping, or otherwise, without the prior written permission of the publisher. No one shall upload this play(s), or part of this play(s), to any social media sites.

CAUTION: Professionals and amateurs are hereby warned that *QUEENS OF FRANCE* is subject to a licensing fee. The amateur and/or professional live stage performance rights to *QUEENS OF FRANCE* are controlled exclusively by Samuel French, Inc. Publication of this play(s) does not imply availability for performance. Both amateurs and professionals considering a production are strongly advised to apply to Samuel French, Inc. before starting rehearsals, advertising, or booking a theatre. A Licensing fee must be paid whether the play(s) is presented for charity or gain and whether or not admission is charged. Professional/Stock licensing fees are quoted upon application to Samuel French, Inc.

Whenever the play(s) is produced the following notice must appear on all programs, printing and advertising for the play(s): "Produced by special arrangement with Samuel French, Inc.

For all other rights than those stipulated above, apply to: The Wilder Family LLC. Visit www.ThorntonWilder.com/resources for details.

MUSIC USE NOTE

Licensees are solely responsible for obtaining formal written permission from copyright owners to use copyrighted music in the performance of this play and are strongly cautioned to do so. If no such permission is obtained by the licensee, then the licensee must use only original music that the licensee owns and controls. Licensees are solely responsible and liable for all music clearances and shall indemnify the copyright owners of the play(s) and their licensing agent, Samuel French, Inc., against any costs, expenses, losses and liabilities arising from the use of music by licensees.

IMPORTANT BILLING AND CREDIT REQUIREMENTS

All producers of *QUEENS OF FRANCE* must give credit to the Author(s) of the Play(s) in all programs distributed in connection with performances of the Play(s), and in all instances in which the title of the Play(s) appears for the purposes of advertising, publicizing or otherwise exploiting the Play(s) and/or a production. The name of the Author(s) *must* appear on a separate line on which no other name appears, immediately following the title and *must* appear in size of type not less than fifty percent of the size of the title type.

INTRODUCTION TO WILDER'S *QUEENS OF FRANCE*

Queens of France is one of six one-act plays that the thirty four-year-old Thornton Wilder published in 1931 – in the United States and in England – under the title, *The Long Christmas Dinner and Other Plays in One Act*. Each play celebrates different theatrical forms and moods. Today, with a bow to their place in twenty-century drama, we call them *Wilder's Classic One Acts*.

Wilder always wanted to write plays – and wasted little time getting started. By the time he had graduated from college in 1920 he had already published some twenty pieces of short drama and one major play (to say nothing of being prodigiously well read in theater, haunting many a stage, and even serving a stint as a paid critic).

But when these six plays appeared, few beyond an inner-circle thought of him as a playwright. (*Our Town*, his first full-length drama to reach Broadway, still lay seven years in the future – opening February 4, 1938.) Everyone, however, knew Thornton Wilder as a novelist – the writer who had given the world three novels, among them the acclaimed 1927 Pulitzer Prize-winning *The Bridge of San Luis Rey*.

Wilder's lack of public status as a dramatist notwithstanding, fans of his fiction and others eagerly purchased his newest offering, and sales of *The Long Christmas Dinner and Other Plays in One Act* were strong. (It could not have hurt sales that the influential *New York Times* reviewer Percy Hutchison found several plays in the volume "very near to miniature masterpieces.") Plays, of course, show best when performed, and after Samuel French added Wilder's titles to its list in 1932, productions began springing up across the country and in England.

Although written for schools and community playhouses, the official record of these plays – with the exception of *Such Things Only Happen in Books*[*], includes professional productions, adaptations for radio, television, and in the case of *The Long Christmas Dinner*, even opera. Perhaps the most high-profile production of any of the six was the successful Broadway run of *The Happy Journey to Trenton and Camden*, performed as a curtain-raiser for Jean-Paul Sartre's *The Respectful Prostitute* in 1947. And given their stature we cannot be surprised that over the past half century, several of the six have turned up regularly off-Broadway, winning critical acclaim and awards.

---

[*] When it was first produced, Wilder described *Such Things Only Happen in Books*, a play he purposely (and playfully) constructed in a conventional form, as "an attempt to see how many plots may be worked into one act." By the late 1930s, for reasons never explained, he had withdrawn it. It remained in this status until 1997 when Wilder's literary executor restored it to the Wilder canon.

Students of American drama have long recognized that these plays contain examples of techniques and devices that Wilder would later employ in his four major plays: *Our Town* (1938), *The Merchant of Yonkers/The Matchmaker* (1938/1954), *The Skin of our Teeth* (1942) and *The Alcestiad* (1955). In these one acts we find Wilder experimenting with such innovative ideas as the stage-manager as a visible and engaged character, non-linear time schemes, the banishment of literal scenery, and elements drawn from farce and Classical theater.

Farce, one of Wilder's lifelong passions, is where *Queens of France* comes in. So it is that we find Molière – a writer Wilder had taught during his stint as a French teacher at Lawrenceville School – all but reborn in 19th century New Orleans. Wilder continued to explore farce in his other works of this period including *The Skin of Our Teeth*, the novel *Heaven's My Destination* (1935) and the Thornton Wilder-Ken Ludwig adaptation of Farquahr's late-Restoration comedy *The Beaux' Strategem* (1939/2006).

When performing Wilder's one acts, actors therefore find themselves handling the theatrical tools that not only contributed to a lasting chapter in the history of twentieth century drama and fiction, but also exploring ancient and honorable theatrical styles.

But the reason for producing these plays is not their role in Thornton Wilder's artistic future, as arresting as that role may be. The enormous success of *Wilder's Classic One Acts* over the years speaks to the more important reason: that these short pieces of drama play wonderfully well in their own right as polished and masterful representatives of drama in the compressed form.

***

Samuel French and the Wilder family take great pleasure and pride in celebrating *Wilder's Classics One Acts*, now in their eighth decade, by reissuing them in new collected and individual acting editions. For additional information about these plays, we invite you to visit www.thorntonwilder.com.

Tappan Wilder
Literary Executor for Thornton Wilder

CHARACTERS

MARIE–SIDONIE CRESSAUX, an attractive young woman.
M'SU CAHUSAC, a lawyer.
MADAME PUGEOT, a plump little bourgeois.
MAMSELLE POINTEVIN, a spinster.
2 extras, **BOY** and **OLD WOMAN.**

SETTING

A lawyer's office in New Orleans, 1869.

(The office door to the street is hung with a reed curtain, through which one obtains a glimpse of a public park in sunshine.)

(A small bell tinkles. After a pause it rings again.)

(MARIE-SIDONIE CRESSAUX pushes the reeds apart and peers in.)

(She is an attractive young woman equal to any situation in life except a summons to a lawyer's office.)

(M'SU CAHUSAC, a dry little man with sharp black eyes, enters from an inner room.)

MARIE-SIDONIE. *(indicating a letter in her hand)* You...you have asked me to come and see you.

M. CAHUSAC. *(severe and brief)* Your name, madame?

MARIE-SIDONIE. Mamselle Marie-Sidonie Cressaux, M'su.

M. CAHUSAC. *(after a pause)* Yes. Kindly be seated, Mamselle.

(He goes to his desk and opens a great many drawers, collecting documents from each. Presently having assembled a large bundle, he returns to the center of the room and says abruptly:)

Mamselle, this interview is to be regarded by you as strictly confidential.

MARIE-SIDONIE. Yes , M'su.

M. CAHUSAC. *(after looking at her sternly a moment:)* May I ask if Mamselle is able to bear the shock of surprise, of good or bad news?

MARIE-SIDONIE. Why...yes, M'su.

M. CAHUSAC. Then if you are Mamselle Marie-Sidonie Cressaux, the daughter of Baptiste-Anténor Cressaux, it is my duty to inform you that you are in danger.

MARIE-SIDONIE. I am in danger, M'su?

(He returns to his desk, opens further drawers, and returns with more papers. She follows him with bewildered eyes.)

M. CAHUSAC. Mamselle, in addition to my duties as a lawyer in this city, I am the representative here of a historical society in Paris. Will you please try and follow me, Mamselle? This historical society has been engaged in tracing the descendants of the true heir to the French throne. As you know, at the time of the Revolution, in 1795, to be exact, Mamselle, the true, lawful, and legitimate heir to the French throne disappeared. It was rumored that this boy, who was then ten years old, came to America and lived for a time in New Orleans. We now know that the rumor was true. We now know that he here begot legitimate issue, that this legitimate issue in turn begot legitimate issue, and that –

(MARIE-SIDONIE suddenly starts searching for something in her shopping bag.)

Mamselle, may I have the honor of your attention a little longer?

MARIE-SIDONIE. *(choking)* My fan – my, my fan, M'su. *(She finds it and at once begins to fan herself wildly. Suddenly she cries out.)* M'su, what danger am I in?

M. CAHUSAC. *(sternly)* If Mamselle will exercise a moment's – one moment's – patience, she will know all...That legitimate issue here begot legitimate issue, and the royal line of France has been traced to a certain *(He consults his documents.)* Baptiste-Anténor Cressaux.

MARIE-SIDONIE. *(Her fan stops and she stares at him.)* Ba't-Ba'tiste!...

M. CAHUSAC. *(leaning forward with menacing emphasis)* Mamselle, can you prove that you are the daughter of Baptiste-Anténor Cressaux?

MARIE-SIDONIE. Why...Why...

M. CAHUSAC. Mamselle, have you a certificate of your parents' marriage?

MARIE-SIDONIE. Yes, M'su.

M. CAHUSAC. If it turns out to be valid, and if it is true that you have no true lawful and legitimate brothers –

MARIE-SIDONIE. No, M'su.

M. CAHUSAC. Then, Mamselle, I have nothing further to do than to announce to you that you are the true and long-lost heir to the throne of France.

(He draws himself up, approaches her with great dignity, and kisses her hand. **MARIE-SIDONIE** *begins to cry. He goes to the desk, pours out a glass of water and, murmuring "Your Royal Highness," offers it to her.)*

MARIE-SIDONIE. M'su Cahusac, I am very sorry...But there must be some mistake. My father was a poor sailor... a...a poor sailor.

M. CAHUSAC. *(reading from his papers)* ...A distinguished and esteemed navigator.

MARIE-SIDONIE. ...A poor sailor...

M. CAHUSAC. *(firmly)* ...Navigator...

(Pause. **MARIE-SIDONIE** *looks about, stricken.)*

MARIE-SIDONIE. *(as before, suddenly and loudly)* M'su, what danger am I in?

M. CAHUSAC. *(approaching her and lowering his voice)* As Your Royal Highness knows, there are several families in New Orleans that claim, without documents *(He rattles the vellum and seals in his hand),* without proof – that pretend to the blood royal. The danger from them, however, is not great. The real danger is from France. From the impassioned Republicans.

MARIE-SIDONIE. Impass...

M. CAHUSAC. But Your Royal Highness has only to put Herself into my hands.

MARIE-SIDONIE. *(crying again)* Please do not call me "Your Royal Highness."

M. CAHUSAC. You...give me permission to call you Madame de Cressaux?

MARIE-SIDONIE. Yes, M'su. Mamselle Cressaux. I am Marie-Sidonie Cressaux.

M. CAHUSAC. Am I mistaken...hmm...in saying that you have children?

MARIE-SIDONIE. *(faintly)* Yes, M'su. I have three children.

(**M. CAHUSAC** *looks at her thoughtfully a moment and returns to his desk.*)

M. CAHUSAC. Madame, from now on thousands of eyes will be fixed upon you, the eyes of the whole world, madame. I cannot urge you too strongly to be very discreet, to be very circumspect.

MARIE-SIDONIE. *(rising, abruptly, nervously)* M'su Cahusac, I do not wish to have anything to do with this. There is a mistake somewhere. I thank you very much, but there is a mistake somewhere. I do not know where. I must go now.

M. CAHUSAC. *(darts forward)* But, Madame, you do not know what you are doing. Your rank cannot be dismissed as easily as that. Do you not know that in a month or two, all the newspapers in the world, including the New Orleans *Times-Picayune*, will publish your name? The first nobles of France will cross the ocean to call upon you. The bishop of Louisiana will call upon you...the mayor...

MARIE-SIDONIE. No, no.

M. CAHUSAC. You will be given a great deal of money and several palaces.

MARIE-SIDONIE. No, no.

M. CAHUSAC. And a guard of soldiers to protect you.

MARIE-SIDONIE. No, no.

M. CAHUSAC. You will be made president of Le Petit Salon and queen of the Mardi Gras...Another sip of water, Your Royal Highness.

MARIE-SIDONIE. Oh, M'su, what shall I do?...Oh, M'su, save me! – I do not want the bishop or the mayor.

M. CAHUSAC. You ask me what you shall do?

MARIE-SIDONIE. Oh, yes, oh, my God!

M. CAHUSAC. For the present, return to your home and lie down. A little rest and a little reflection will tell you what you have to do. Then come and see me Thursday morning.

MARIE-SIDONIE. I think there must be a mistake somewhere.

M. CAHUSAC. May I be permitted to ask Madame de Cressaux a question: Could I have the privilege of presenting Her – until the great announcement takes place – with a small gift of...money?

MARIE-SIDONIE. No, no.

M. CAHUSAC. The historical society is not rich. The historical society has difficulty in pursuing the search for the last documents that will confirm madame's exalted rank, but they would be very happy to advance a certain sum to madame, subscribed by her devoted subjects.

MARIE-SIDONIE. Please no. I do not wish any. I must go now.

M. CAHUSAC. Let me beg madame not to be alarmed. For the present a little rest and reflection...

(The bell rings. He again bends over her hand, murmuring "...obedient servant and devoted subject....")

MARIE-SIDONIE. *(in confusion)* Good-bye, good morning, M. Cahusac. *(She lingers at the door a moment, then returns and says in great earnestness:)* Oh, M. Cahusac, do not let the bishop come and see me. The mayor, yes – but not the bishop.

(Enter **MADAME PUGEOT,** *a plump little bourgeoise in black. Exit* **MARIE-SIDONIE.** **M. CAHUSAC** *kisses the graciously extended hand of* **MADAME PUGEOT.**)

MME. PUGEOT. Good morning, M. Cahusac.

M. CAHUSAC. Your Royal Highness.

MME. PUGEOT. What business can you possibly be having with that dreadful Marie Cressaux! Do you not know that she is an abandoned woman?

M. CAHUSAC. Alas, we are in the world, Your Royal Highness. For the present I must earn a living as best I can. Mamselle Cressaux is arranging about the purchase of a house and garden.

MME. PUGEOT. Purchase, M. Cahusac, phi! You know very well that she has half a dozen houses and gardens already. She persuades every one of her lovers to give her a little house and garden. She is beginning to own the whole parish of Saint-Magloire.

M. CAHUSAC. Will Your Royal Highness condescend to sit down? *(She does.)* And how is the royal family this morning?

MME. PUGEOT. Only so-so, M'su Cahusac.

M. CAHUSAC. The Archduchess of Tuscany?

MME. PUGEOT. *(fanning herself with a turkey's wing)* A cold. One of her colds. I sometimes think the dear child will never live to see her pearls.

M. CAHUSAC. And the Dauphin, Your Royal Highness?

MME. PUGEOT. Still, still amusing himself in the city, as young men will. Wine, gambling, bad company. At least it keeps him out of harm.

M. CAHUSAC. And the Duke of Burgundy?

MME. PUGEOT. Imagine! The poor child has a sty in his eye!

M. CAHUSAC. Tchk-tchk! *(with solicitude)* In which eye, madame?

MME. PUGEOT. In the left!

M. CAHUSAC. Tchk-tchk! And the Prince of Lorraine and the Duke of Berry?

MME. PUGEOT. They are fairly well, but they seem to mope in their cradle. Their first teeth, my dear chamberlain.

M. CAHUSAC. And your husband, madame?

MME. PUGEOT. *(rises, walks back and forth a moment, then stands still)* From now on we are never to mention him again – while we are discussing these matters. It is to be understood that he is my husband in a manner of speaking only. He has no part in my true life. He has chosen to scoff at my birth and my rank, but he will see what he will see...Naturally I have not told him about the proofs that you and I have collected. I have not the heart to let him see how unimportant he will become.

M. CAHUSAC. Unimportant, indeed!

MME. PUGEOT. So remember, we do not mention him in the same breath *with these matters!*

M. CAHUSAC. You must trust me, Madame. *(softly, with significance)* And *your* health, Your Royal Highness?

MME. PUGEOT. Oh, very well, thank you. Excellent. I used to do quite poorly, as you remember, but since this wonderful news I have been more than well, God be praised.

M. CAHUSAC. *(as before, with lifted eyebrows)* I beg of you to do nothing unwise. I beg of you...The little new life we are all anticipating...

MME. PUGEOT. Have no fear, my dear chamberlain. What is dear to France is dear to me.

M. CAHUSAC. When I think, madame, of how soon we shall be able to announce your rank – when I think that this time next year you will be enjoying all the honors and privileges that are your due, I am filled with a pious joy.

MME. PUGEOT. God's will be done, God's will be done.

M. CAHUSAC. At all events, I am particularly happy to see that Your Royal Highness is in the best of health, for I have had a piece of disappointing news.

MME. PUGEOT. Chamberlain, you are not going to tell me that Germany has at last declared war upon my country?

M. CAHUSAC. No, madame.

MME. PUGEOT. You greatly frightened me last week. I could scarcely sleep. Such burdens as I have! My husband tells me that I cried out in my sleep the words: *"Paris, I come!"*

M. CAHUSAC. Sublime, Madame!

MME. PUGEOT. *"Paris, I come,"* like that. I cried out twice in my sleep: *"Paris, I come."* Oh, these are anxious times; I am on my way to the cathedral now. This Bismarck does not understand me. We must avoid a war at all costs, M. Cahusac...Then what is your news?

M. CAHUSAC. My anxiety at present is more personal. The historical society in Paris is now confirming the last proofs of your claim. They have secretaries at work in all the archives: Madrid, Vienna, Constantinople...

MME. PUGEOT. Constantinople!

M. CAHUSAC. All this requires a good deal of money and the society is not rich. We have been driven to a painful decision. The society must sell one of the royal jewels or one of the royal *fournitures* which I am guarding upstairs. The historical society has written me, Madame, ordering me to send them at once – the royal christening robe.

MME. PUGEOT. Never!

M. CAHUSAC. The very robe under which Charlemagne was christened, the Charles, the Henris, the Louis, to lie under a glass in the Louvre. *(softly)* And this is particularly painful to me because I had hoped – it was, in fact, the dream of my life – to see at least one of your children christened under all those fleurs-de-lis.

MME. PUGEOT. It shall not go to the Louvre. I forbid it.

M. CAHUSAC. But what can I do? I offered them the scepter. I offered them the orb. I even offered them the mug which Your Royal Highness has already purchased. But no! The christening robe it must be.

MME. PUGEOT. It shall not leave America! *(clutching her handbag)* How much are they asking for it?

M. CAHUSAC. Oh, madame, since it is the Ministry of Museums and Monuments they are asking a great many thousands of francs.

MME. PUGEOT. And how much would they ask their Queen?

M. CAHUSAC. *(sadly)* Madame, Madame, I cannot see you purchasing those things which are rightly yours.

MME. PUGEOT. I will purchase it. I shall sell the house on the Chausée Sainte Anne.

M. CAHUSAC. *(softly)* If Your Majesty will give five hundred dollars of Her money I shall add five hundred of my own.

MME. PUGEOT. *(shaken)* Five hundred. Five hundred...Well, you will be repaid many times, my dear chamberlain, when I am restored to my position *(she thinks a moment)* Tomorrow at three. I shall bring you the papers for the sale of the house. You will do everything quietly. My husband will be told about it in due time.

M. CAHUSAC. I understand. I shall be very discreet.

(The bell rings. **M. CAHUSAC** *turns to the door as* **MAMSELLE POINTEVIN** *starts to enter.)*

I shall be free to see you in a few moments, Mamselle. Madame Pugeot has still some details to discuss with me.

MLLE. POINTEVIN. I cannot wait long, M'su Cahusac.

M. CAHUSAC. A few minutes in the park, thank you, Mamselle.

(Exit **MAMSELLE POINTEVIN**.*)*

MME. PUGEOT. Has that poor girl business with a lawyer, M. Cahusac? A poor schoolteacher like that?

M. CAHUSAC. *(softly)* Mamselle Pointevin has taken it into her head to make her will.

MME. PUGEOT. *(laughs superiorly)* Three chairs and a broken plate. *(rising)* Well, tomorrow at three...I am now going to the cathedral. I do not forget the great responsibilities for which I must prepare myself-the army, the navy, the treasury, the appointment of bishops. When I am dead, my dear chamberlain –

M. CAHUSAC. Madame!

MME. PUGEOT. O, no! – even I must die some day...When I am dead, when I am laid with my ancestors, let it never be said of me...By the way, where shall I be laid?

M. CAHUSAC. In the church of Saint Denis, Your Royal Highness?

MME. PUGEOT. Not in Notre Dame?

M. CAHUSAC. No, madame.

MME. PUGEOT. *(meditatively)* Not in Notre Dame. Well *(brightening)* we will cross these bridges when we get to them. *(extending her hand)* Good morning and all my thanks, my dear chamberlain.

M. CAHUSAC. ...Highness's most obedient servant and devoted subject.

MME. PUGEOT. *(beautifully filling the doorway)* Pray for us.

(Exit **MADAME PUGEOT.** **M. CAHUSAC** *goes to the door and bows to* **MAMSELLE POINTEVIN** *in the street.)*

M. CAHUSAC. Now Mamselle, if you will have the goodness to enter.

(Enter **MAMSELLE POINTEVIN,** *a tall and indignant spinster.)*

MLLE. POINTEVIN. M'su Cahusac, it is something new for you to keep me waiting in the public square while you carry on your wretched little business with a vulgar woman like Madame Pugeot. When I condescend to call upon you, my good man, you will have the goodness to receive me at once. Either I am, or I am not, Henriette, Queen of France, Queen of Navarre and Aquitania. It is not fitting that we cool our heels on a public bench among the nursemaids of remote New Orleans. It is hard enough for me to hide myself as a schoolmistress in this city, without having to suffer further humiliations at your hands. Is there no respect due to the blood of Charlemagne?

M. CAHUSAC. Madame...

MLLE. POINTEVIN. Or, sir, are you bored and overfed on the company of queens?

M. CAHUSAC. Madame...

MLLE. POINTEVIN. You are busy with the law. Good! Know, then, La loi-c'est moi. *(sitting down and smoothing out her skirts)* Now what is it you have to say?

M. CAHUSAC. *(pauses a moment, then approaches her with tightly pressed lips and narrowed eyes)* Your Royal Highness, I have received a letter from France. There is some discouraging news.

MLLE. POINTEVIN. No! I cannot afford to buy another thing. I possess the scepter and the orb. Sell the rest to the Louvre, if you must. I can buy them back when my rank is announced.

M. CAHUSAC. Alas!

MLLE. POINTEVIN. What do you mean "alas"?

M. CAHUSAC. Will Your Royal Highness condescend to read the letter I have received from France?

MLLE. POINTEVIN. *(unfurls the letter, but continues looking before her, splendidly)* Have they no bread? Give them cake. *(She starts to read, is shaken, suddenly returns it to him.)* It is too long. It is too long...What does it say?

M. CAHUSAC. It is from the secretary of the historical society. The society remains convinced that you are the true and long-sought heir to the throne of France.

MLLE. POINTEVIN. Convinced? Convinced? I should hope so.

M. CAHUSAC. But to make this conviction public, madame, to announce it throughout the newspapers of the world, including the New Orleans *Times-Picayune*...

MLLE. POINTEVIN. Yes, go on!

M. CAHUSAC. To establish your claim among all your rivals. To establish your claim beyond any possible ridicule...

MLLE. POINTEVIN. Ridicule!

M. CAHUSAC. All they lack is one little document. One little but important document. They had hoped to find it in the archives of Madrid. Madame, it is not there.

MLLE. POINTEVIN. It is not there? Then where is it?

M. CAHUSAC. We do not know, Your Royal Highness. We are in despair.

MLLE. POINTEVIN. Ridicule, M. Cahusac!

(She stares at him, her hand on her mouth.)

M. CAHUSAC. It may be in Constantinople. It may be in Vienna. Naturally we shall continue to search for it. We shall continue to search for generations, for centuries, if need be. But I must confess this is a very discouraging blow.

MLLE. POINTEVIN. Generations! Centuries! But I am not a young girl, M'su Cahusac. Their letter says over and over again that I am the heir to the throne. *(She begins to cry.)*

*(**M. CAHUSAC** discreetly offers her a glass of water.)*

Thank you.

M. CAHUSAC. *(suddenly changing his tone, with firmness)* Madame, you should know that the society suspects the lost document to be in your possession. The society feels sure that the document has been handed down from generation to generation in your family.

MLLE. POINTEVIN. In my possession!

M. CAHUSAC. *(firmly)* Madame, are you concealing something from us?

MLLE. POINTEVIN. Why...no.

M. CAHUSAC. Are you playing with us, as a cat plays with a mouse?

MLLE. POINTEVIN. No indeed I'm not.

M. CAHUSAC. Why is that paper not in Madrid, or in Constantinople or in Vienna? Because it is in your house. You live in what was once your father's house, do you not?

MLLE. POINTEVIN. Yes, I do.

M. CAHUSAC. Go back to it. Look through every old trunk...

MLLE. POINTEVIN. Every old trunk!

M. CAHUSAC. Examine especially the linings. Look through all the tables and desks. Pry into the joints. You will find perhaps a secret drawer, a secret panel.

MLLE. POINTEVIN. M'su Cahusac!

M. CAHUSAC. Examine the walls. Examine the boards of the floor. It may be hidden beneath them.

MLLE. POINTEVIN. I will. I'll go now.

M. CAHUSAC. Have you any old clothes of your father?

MLLE. POINTEVIN. Yes, I have.

M. CAHUSAC. It may be sewn into the lining.

MLLE. POINTEVIN. I'll look.

M. CAHUSAC. Madame, in what suit of clothes was your father buried?

MLLE. POINTEVIN. In his best, M'su.

(She gives a sudden scream under her hand as this thought strikes home. They stare at one another significantly.)

M. CAHUSAC. Take particular pains to look under all steps. These kinds of documents are frequently found under steps. You will find it. If it is not in Madrid, it is there.

MLLE. POINTEVIN. But if I can't find it! *(She sits down, suddenly spent.)* No one will ever know that I am the Queen of France. *(pause)* I am very much afraid, M'su Cahusac, that I shall never find that document in my four rooms. I know every inch of them. But I shall look. *(She draws her hand across her forehead, as though awaking from a dream.)* It is all very strange. You know, M'su Cahusac, I think there may have been a mistake somewhere. It was so beautiful while it lasted. It made even school teaching a pleasure, M'su...And my memoirs. I have just written my memoirs up to the moment when your wonderful announcement came to me – the account of my childhood incognito, the little girl in Louisiana who did not guess the great things before her. But before I go, may I ask something of you? Will you have the historical society write me a letter saying that they seriously think I may be…the person…the person they are looking for? I wish to keep the letter in the trunk with the orb and…with the scepter. You know…the more I think of it, the more I think there must have been a mistake somewhere.

M. CAHUSAC. The very letter you have in mind is here, madame.

(He gives it to her.)

MLLE. POINTEVIN. Thank you. And M'su Cahusac, may I ask another favor of you?

M. CAHUSAC. Certainly, madame.

MLLE. POINTEVIN. Please, never mention this…this whole affair to anyone in New Orleans.

M. CAHUSAC. Madame, not unless you wish it.

MLLE. POINTEVIN. Good morning – good morning, and thank you. *(Her handkerchief to one eye, she goes out.)*

*(**M. CAHUSAC** goes to his desk.)*

*(The bell rings. The reed curtain is parted and a **NEGRO BOY** pushes in a wheelchair containing a **WOMAN** of some hundred years of age. She is wrapped in shawls, like a mummy, and wears a scarf about her head, and green spectacles on her nose. The mummy extends a hand which **M. CAHUSAC** kisses devotedly, murmuring, "Your Royal Highness.")*

End of Play

ABOUT THORNTON WILDER

Born in Madison, Wisconsin, and educated at Yale and Princeton, Thornton Wilder (1897-1975) was an accomplished novelist and playwright whose works explore the connection between the commonplace and the cosmic dimensions of human experience. *The Bridge of San Luis Rey*, one of his seven novels, won the Pulitzer Prize in 1928, and his next-to-last novel, *The Eighth Day* received the National Book Award (1968). Two of his four major plays garnered Pulitzer Prizes, *Our Town* (1938) and *The Skin of Our Teeth* (1943). His play, *The Matchmaker* ran on Broadway for 486 performances (1955-1957), Wilder's Broadway record, and was later adapted into the musical *Hello, Dolly!* Wilder also enjoyed enormous success with many other forms of the written and spoken word, among them translation, acting, opera librettos, lecturing, teaching and film (his screenplay for Alfred Hitchcock's 1943 psycho-thriller, *Shadow of a Doubt* remains a classic to this day). Letter writing held a central place in Wilder's life, and since his death, three volumes of his letters have been published. Wilder's many honors include the Gold Medal for Fiction from the American Academy of Arts and Letters, the Presidential Medal of Freedom, and the National Book Committee's Medal for Literature. On April 17, 1997, the centenary of his birth, the US Postal Service unveiled the Thornton Wilder 32-cent stamp in Hamden, Connecticut, his official address after 1930 and where he died on December 7, 1975.

For more information, visit www.thorntonwilder.com.

Also by
Thornton Wilder...

The Alcestiad
The Beaux' Stratagem (with Ken Ludwig)
The Matchmaker
Our Town
The Skin of Our Teeth

<u>Thornton Wilder One Act Series: The Ages of Man</u>
Infancy
Childhood
Youth
Rivers Under the Earth

<u>Thornton Wilder One Act Series: The Seven Deadly Sins</u>
The Drunken Sisters
Bernice
The Wreck on the 5:25
A Ringing of Doorbells
In Shakespeare and the Bible
Someone From Assisi
Cement Hands

<u>Thornton Wilder One Act Series: Wilder's Classic One Acts</u>
The Long Christmas Dinner
Queens of France
Pullman Car Hiawatha
Love and How to Cure It
Such Things Only Happen in Books
The Happy Journey to Trenton and Camden

Please visit our website **samuelfrench.com** for complete descriptions and licensing information.

OTHER TITLES AVAILABLE FROM SAMUEL FRENCH

THE SKIN OF OUR TEETH

Thornton Wilder

Comedy / 4 or 5m, 4 or 5f, plus many small parts w/doubling / Interior, Exterior

Winner of the 1943 Pulitzer Prize for Drama

Completed by the author less than a month after the Japanese attack on Pearl Harbor on December 7, 1941, *The Skin of Our Teeth* (1942) broke from established theatrical conventions and walked off with the 1943 Pulitzer Prize for Drama. Combining farce, burlesque, and satire, and elements of the comic strip, Thornton Wilder depicts an Everyman Family as it narrowly escapes one end-of-the-world disaster after another, from the Ice Age to flood to war.

Meet George and Maggie Antrobus of Excelsior, New Jersey, a suburban, commuter-town couple (married for 5,000 years), who bear more than a casual resemblance to that first husband and wife, Adam and Eve: the two Antrobus children, Gladys (perfect in every way, of course) and Henry (who likes to throw rocks and was formerly known as Cain); and their garrulous maid, Sabina (the eternal seductress), who takes it upon herself to break out of character and interrupt the course of the drama at every opportunity ("I don't understand a word of this play!")

Whether he is inventing the alphabet or merely saving the world from apocalypse, George and his redoubtable family somehow manage to survive – by the skin of their teeth.

"For an American dramatist, all roads lead back to Thornton Wilder...*The Skin of Our Teeth* was a remarkable gift to an America entrenched in catastrophe, a tribute to the trait of human endurance."
– Paula Vogel, "Foreword", *The Skin of Our Teeth*

SAMUELFRENCH.COM

www.ingramcontent.com/pod-product-compliance
Lightning Source LLC
Chambersburg PA
CBHW071419290426
44108CB00014B/1888